DEDICATION

This book is dedicated to:

Virginia Hummel (MA)

John Hummel (PA)

Dennis R. Paschall

MM Garner, Jr.

And

Isham Gathright.

This page is meant to be a blank

This page is meant to be a blank

This page is meant to be a blank

This page is meant to be a blank

This page is meant to be a blank

This page is meant to be a blank

This page is meant to be a blank

This page is meant to be a blank

This page is meant to be a blank

This page is meant to be a blank

This page is meant to be a blank

PLEASE
PRAY FOR
THOSE
WHO
STRUGGLE
WITH
BREAST
CANCER OR
ANY KIND
OF
CANCER.

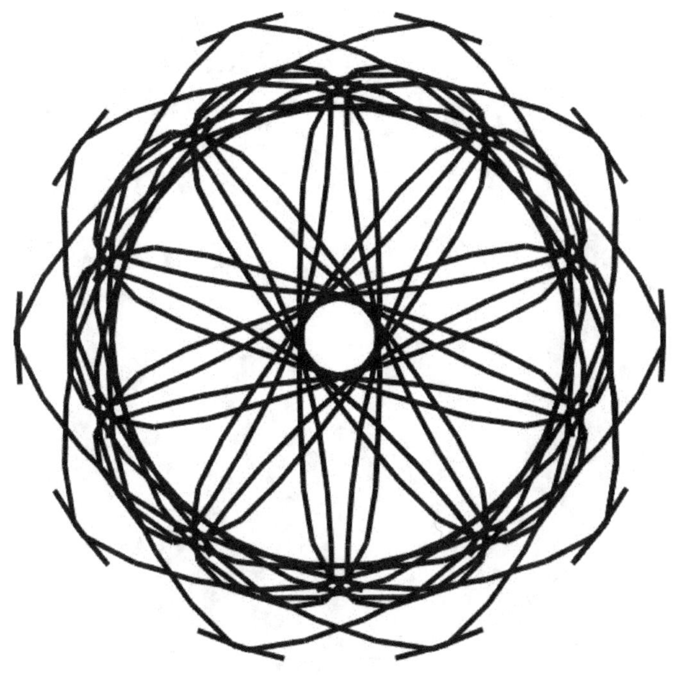

This page is meant to be a blank

This page is meant to be a blank

SUPPORT
LUPUS

This page is meant to be a blank

This page is meant to be a blank

This page is meant to be a blank

This page is meant to be a blank

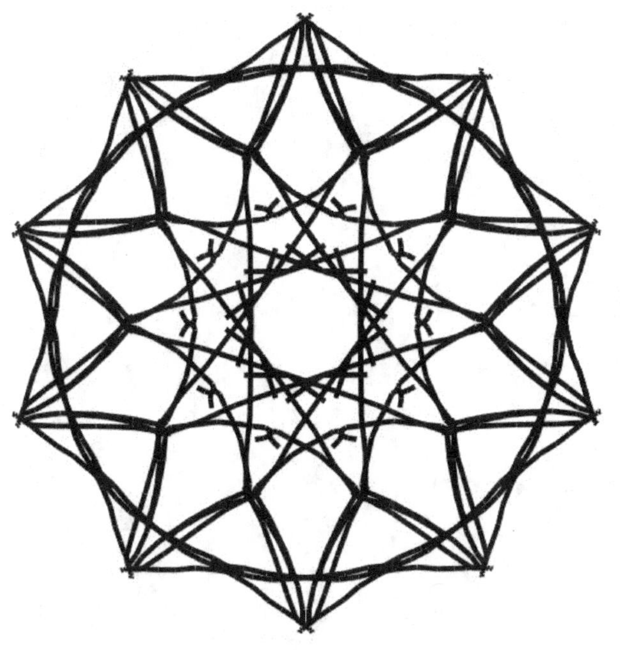

This page is meant to be a blank

This page is meant to be a blank

This page is meant to be a blank

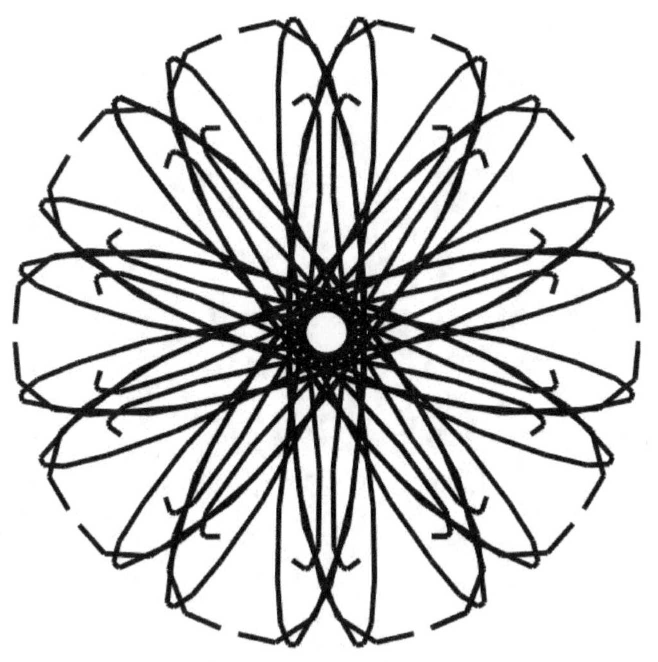

This page is meant to be a blank

This page is meant to be a blank

This page is meant to be a blank

This page is meant to be a blank

This page is meant to be a blank

This page is meant to be a blank

This page is meant to be a blank

This page is meant to be a blank

This page is meant to be a blank

This page is meant to be a blank

This page is meant to be a blank

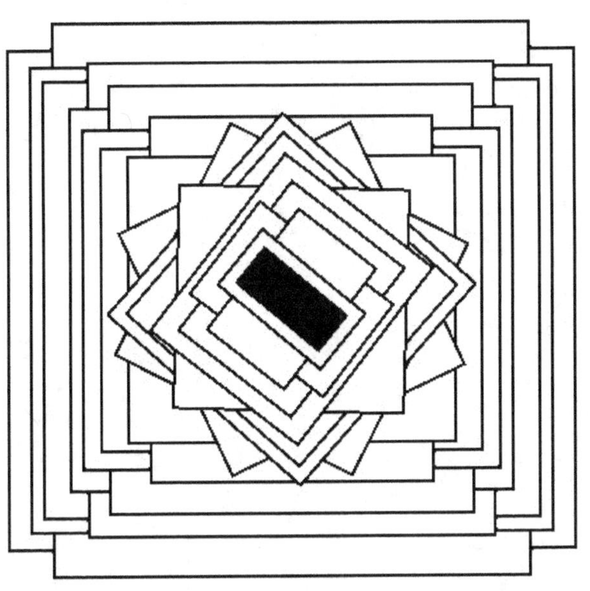

This page is meant to be a blank